DIALOGUE OF THE HEART AND MIND

Enjoy Dialogue

Lou Carla Mitchell

DIALOGUE OF THE HEART AND MIND

Thoughts on Love and Relationships

Carla M. Mitchell

iUniverse, Inc.

New York Lincoln Shanghai

DIALOGUE OF THE HEART AND MIND
Thoughts on Love and Relationships

iUniverse books may be ordered through booksellers or by contacting:

iUniverse
2021 Pine Lake Road, Suite 100
Lincoln, NE 68512
www.iuniverse.com
1-800-Authors (1-800-288-4677)

Because of the dynamic nature of the Internet, any Web addresses or links contained in this book may have changed since publication and may no longer be valid.

The views expressed in this work are solely those of the author and do not necessarily reflect the views of the publisher, and the publisher hereby disclaims any responsibility for them.

ISBN: 978-0-595-43502-9 (pbk)
ISBN: 978-0-595-69482-2 (cloth)
ISBN: 978-0-595-87828-4 (ebk)

Printed in the United States of America

CONTENTS

Foreword to
A Dialogue of the Heart & Mind
Frank A. Thomas

When I read Carla Mitchell's work, "A Dialogue of the Heart & Mind," I wondered why there were not more books like this that speak with honesty and integrity about quality Christian relationships between male and females. While we have many books on relationships, I long most for books that are honest, direct, and scripturally based. There is often in many books on relationships an avoidance of what I call "the real." Writers escape into a kind of Christian piety that denies the true agony of suffering and heartbreak and ends up giving easy and predictable answers to the deep and complex questions of life. These kinds of books ignore the hard and gut-wrenching choices of dating, pre-marital sex, divorce, self-esteem issues, etc. and offer people Bible-based "shoulds and oughts." When something is on "the real," we honestly face the difficulties of pain and suffering, we accept the pain and suffering with a tremendous amount of humility, and we look for responses of grace from God (not answers) in Scripture. Carla Mitchell discusses "the real" of relationships.

Another way to say the same thing is out of the four principle realities of life—God, love, power, and sex. The church speaks loudly and often about God and love. We do not very often talk about power and sex and power and sex is where most of us make the majority of our relationship mistakes. Many people are looking for straight-forward, Christian-based discussion about the reality of power and sex in relationships. Carla Mitchell has seen this need and met it.

I believe the role of the church is to teach Biblical principles on healthy relationships, then facilitate a dialogue. For too long have people mouthed Scripture, but lived an entirely different reality from that which the Bible says. Many people will come to church and assent to what the Bible teaches and then walk out and behave opposite of what they just heard. The addition of discussion and dialogue to the lessons of Scripture allows us to close the gap between what we say we believe and what we actually do. As a matter of fact, I pay less attention to what people say they believe and more attention to what they do. Carla Mitchell facilitates the discussion and dialogue that allows the reader to close the gap between what they say they believe and what they do.

Hence, the real purpose of this book is about self-discovery and self honesty before God. The book is a reason to examine ourselves, our assumptions, and our behavior and close the gap between what we say and what we do. But it starts with unbending honesty with oneself as one's relationship needs and motives. Do we really have the courage to be by ourselves? Can we really be with another if we have not had the courage to be by ourselves? Does the word "relationship" mean the same thing to everyone? Do we settle for pat and easy answers or do we journey with God to do the hard work of finding our own unique calling and purpose in life?

I believe you will be challenged and encouraged to discover God in your journey and your story. God is with you and God is leading you to a life of purpose and destiny. Carla Mitchell will be a coach and facilitator for your deeper discovery. Not only do I suggest that you purchase this book, I suggest that you buy an extra for a friend.

It will help you facilitate the dialogue. I certainly will share it with many, many people in my life and ministry.

Pastor Frank A. Thomas, Sr.

ACKNOWLEDGEMENTS
&
SPECIAL THANKS

First and foremost I must give thanks to my Lord & Savior Jesus Christ for putting it on my heart to write this book. I thank Him for the gift of writing and for the quiet times in which to put my thoughts onto paper … or in this day and age … into a computer.

Thank you to my parents, Thomas Earl & Christine Ervin Mitchell who through their nearly fifty years of marriage have allowed me and my brothers to see that love truly can endureth all things. I'm forever thankful that you have never given up on each other or on Thomas Jr., Kenneth or me. An extra special thanks to you Mom, for both your time and expertise in both proofing and editing this book. Thanks for always insisting that if I was going to do something, I always do my best and give it my all.

To Joy Jones, I'm forever grateful to you for granting me permission to include your article in this book. You truly speak from the heart and with this and other articles you have written, give all of us much to think about.

Pastor Frank A. Thomas, thank you for the awesome Forward you wrote for this book! You got exactly what I was trying to say through this book, which was confirmation that my voice was worth hearing. Thank you also for your teachings and powerful sermons. It was your ministry at New Faith Baptist Church in Matteson, Illinois that helped me develop a path years ago to begin the process to look at, face, accept and when needed change my own stuff.

Elaine Young, Graphic Designer, Art Director and Owner of Hopscotch Communications.com who took my vision for the cover of this book and made it not only real, but awesome! You do amazing work!

To everyone who shared their thoughts about the article, thank you for your honesty, openness and willingness to share. Thanks also for not holding back!

CHAPTER 1

▼

LET THE DIALOGUE BEGIN

A girlfriend sent me a copy of an article entitled, *"Are Black Women Scaring off Our Men?"* It was written by Joy Jones and originally appeared in the "Washington Post" in October, 2005. Well, as someone who's always been interested in the dynamics of relationships, I was eager to read it, and I have to say it gave me some things to think about.

While I can certainly understand Ms. Jones' position, let's first acknowledge that she doesn't speak for all women, or all Black women for that matter, since the title of her article asks if we (Black women) are scaring off our (Black) men? I do think she is asking (Black) women (and this could really be applied to ALL women) to look at ourselves and do some serious soul searching to see if there are parts of our personality that may be sabotaging our relationships with our men.

I've read numerous books on relationships everything from *"Men are from Mars—Women are from Venus,"* by Dr. John Gray; *"If Men are Like Buses, Then How Do I Catch One,"* by Michelle McKinney Hammond; and *"Love Must Be Tough,"* by James Dobson. They're all good books and very different; yet I was able to get something out of each of them. However, very often books like these are based upon one person's observation, perspective or experience.

A few folks asked me, "What's up with you and this article ~ relationship thing?" Honestly, nothing is up! As I stated earlier, I have always been interested in the dynamics of interpersonal relationships. I love and cherish all of my relationships with my family, girlfriends, guy-friends, co-workers, and that "special guy."

So, just how do you define "relationships"? The Merriam-Webster Dictionary defines relationships as: "The state of being related to or interrelated" … Okay?! They then define the word "relation" to be: "A connection connected by blood, marriage or kinship. The state of being mutually interested or involved (as in social matters)." Oh, and their final definition under relation is "sexual intercourse."

Before we go any further, ask yourself this question (see if you've ever been or are guilty of doing this ... I admit, I have): Do you or have you ever "assumed" you were in a relationship with someone, yet neither of you ever took the time to discuss if you both believed you were in a relationship (or wanted to be) or to learn what that word "relationship" meant to the other person or to you?

A male friend and I had a discussion on this very topic, and I think he was on point about people (probably more often women) "assuming" they were in relationships with someone! First question: What makes us think we're in a relationship? Let's take it one step further, what makes us think we're in a "committed-monogamous relationship with someone? Why, because you've slept with them? Gone out on a few dates? Too often, critical issues get tossed aside during the initial development stage of relationships due to gaps (and differences) in communication skills and styles and pre-determined (and often unspoken) expectations. One's judgment almost always gets clouded when you sleep together too early in the "formation" of a potential relationship. This act often causes people (yes, mostly women) to falsely assume we're in a "relationship," and let's be honest, too often we become assumptive in believing we're in a "committed and monogamous" relationship without ever discussing this with the man with whom we believe we're in the committed relationship. We just assume we are and that can often lead to heartache and wasted time and energy!

So, this leads to my next question: Does the word "relationship" mean the same thing to everyone? Probably not. Heck, do relationships even mean the same thing to men and women? Likely not! The reality is that men and women both need to take the time early in the formation of a potential relationship to dig deep, several layers deep to come to a verbal and mutual understanding about what the word "relationship" means to our (perceived) partner, and to gain understanding and agreement on what each other's expectations are about the relationship. Next, we have to ask, "Are these expectations reasonable? Further still, once we hear and clearly understand the other person's expectations, we must ask ourselves, "Am I willing to live up to these expectations?"

I think the same holds true about getting clarity and understanding on how the other person feels about and interprets the following words:

- Family

- Living together

- Commitment & Marriage

- Honor & Trust

- Religion

- Intimacy

CHAPTER 2

▼

WHAT'S THE DEAL

OK, so what's the deal with this book? Why should you spend your hard earned money to purchase it and then give up some of your precious free/down time to read it? Great questions, I'm glad you asked! Here's why:

1. It's an easy read and well worth the money!

2. It was written simply with the hope that men and women would read it and begin doing some self examination.

I know, I know, people hate looking at their own stuff, their own shortcomings, whatever; but if we are unwilling to examine ourselves, to take the time to learn who we are, what we want, what we like and what we're willing to compromise on, how can any of us expect someone with whom we want to be close to in a relationship to be open and honest with us?

3. Use this as a catalyst to have some honest and open dialogue between men and women.

I am the first to say I don't have any answers, nor am I anybody's expert in the field or study of relationships. I do know that it's important to be honest with you, about yourself. I do know that there are too many women walking this earth with their lives virtually on hold because they don't have a man. I also know that life is way too short to put your life on hold for a "maybe"!

Here's what I do know: 1. There are some wonderful heterosexual African American Brothers who truly love their African American Sisters and want to be in committed relationships with them. 2. There are also some wonderful heterosexual men (of all races and ethnic groups) who want a loving relationship with a woman (regardless of race and ethnicity) who will appreciate, respect and cherish them. So perhaps Black women need to be more willing to "think outside of our proverbial relationship box"! I'm in no way saying to give up on our brothers, but if you can't find one who "moves you," then at least be open to date outside of your "racial" comfort zone. We know many, many Black men are doing just that.

CHAPTER 3

▼

TALK BACK TIME

After reading Ms. Jones' article, I sent it on to numerous friends, colleagues and associates. Many of these people shared the article with their friends and were kind enough to share the responses they received with me. I had no clue that so many people would reply to me with their thoughts, or that so many of the responses on the article would be ... so what's the word ... passionate! I even hosted a "Sister-Girl" session at my home, and we ate (what's a "Sister Girl" session without food) and discussed the article, but more about that later! The responses to this article literally took on a life of its own to be quite honest.

Initially, I sent the article to single folks. This group was comprised of folks who were divorced, separated (although let's face it, they're still technically & legally married) and folks who've never been married.

In many cases, the responses were split down the middle. Many of the women did not agree with Ms. Jones and took issue with her implying that women need to be the ones that make the adjustments-changes to be in a satisfying and loving relationship. Specifically, they didn't like her statement, "You may have to stoop to conquer or yield to win." To be honest, I, too, thought that statement was a bit extreme, because no one should have to lower themselves ("stoop") or down play their accomplishments or who they are in order to maintain or even have a relationship! There must be compromises in all relationships from both parties in the relationship. Neither the men nor women with whom I talked or who commented about the article, agreed with that statement of having to "stoop to conquer." Thank goodness!

Interestingly, many of the men felt Ms. Jones was "right on point" and most of the men stated they are not intimidated by women who make more money than they do. Now various writings that have come out over the years have indicated otherwise, but we'll deal with the responses received.

It was later suggested that I obtain responses from married folks. After all, married folks have a different perspective about relationships, and sure enough, they didn't disappoint!

Married folks were very willing to share their thoughts on what they believe is needed to have a successful marriage, and I truly appreciate their honesty and openness.

I believe that across the board, regardless of race or age, relationships are hard work; they require effort, attention, mutual respect, and the desire to make them work ... period!

In reading the responses from the married folks, it appears they still struggle with this, and I do take some comfort in this. At least it confirms what I've believed for some time ... maintaining healthy and successful relationships and marriages is a continuous work in progress! Don't get me wrong, if you're blessed enough to find that special someone and you both put forth the effort to make the marriage work and hang in through the good and bad, the ups and downs, it's worth it!

In all, I personally sent the article to about fifty people and many of those people sent it on to their family, friends and acquaintances. Most of the responses were very simple, brief and direct saying they agreed with Ms. Jones, or that she was on point, she was totally wrong or that she was too generalized in her thoughts about Black women. I received detailed responses from thirty people, twenty eight in writing and two verbally. A couple of the ones who responded in writing sent multiple responses stating that as they thought more about the article and themselves, their opinions about the article changed and they wanted to communicate that. These were rare, but they did occur. Two people called me and wanted to discuss (dialogue) this real time, however, those comments are not included here as I didn't feel I could accurately state their feelings (and not interject my thoughts) as I'd be "interpreting" what I thought I heard them say, rather than stating it exactly as they said it.

I've included all twenty-eight responses in this book and with the exception of some grammatical or spelling corrections the responses are exactly as I received them. Here is the break-down of the respondents:

Total number of respondents—Twenty-eight

- Number of men—Twelve

- Number of women—Sixteen

Break down by Marital Status:

- Number of Singles—Seven

- Number of Divorced—Nine

- Number of Married—Eleven

- Number of Separated—One

Does the number of folks responding represent a good majority of folks available to respond? Nope! But that said I do believe they represent a fair cross section of people, and it is hoped that after you read the article and the responses in this book, you'll share your thoughts and comments too. I'd love to hear from you.

Listen, just enjoy it. Allow your mind to be open and be willing to accept that people don't have to even agree with your way of thinking or interpreting this article or your view of relationships and what they should or should not be. That's OK ... in fact that's great. We're all different and it is those God-ordained differences that are suppose to make each of us unique ... Right?

CHAPTER 4

▼

THE ARTICLE THAT BEGAN THE DIALOGUE

Are Black Women Scaring Off Their Men? (A Fighting Spirit Is Important, But Not At Home)
—*The Washington Post* By: Joy Jones

Have you met this woman? She has a good job, works hard, and earns a good salary. She went to college, she got her master's degree, she is intelligent. She is personable, articulate, well read, interested in everybody and everything. Yet, she's single.

Or maybe you know this one. Active in the church. Faithful, committed, sings in the choir, serves on the usher board, and attends every committee meeting. Loves the Lord and knows the Word. You'd think that with her command of the Scriptures and the respect of her church members, she'd have a marriage as solid as a rock. But again, no husband.

Or, perhaps you recognize the community activist. She's a black lady, or, as she prefers, an African American woman on the move. She sports a short natural; sometimes cornrow braids, or even dreadlocks. She's an organizer, a motivator, a dynamo. Her work for her people speaks for itself—organizing women for self-help, raising funds for a community cause, educating others around a new issue in South Africa. Black folks look up to her, and white folks know she's a force to be reckoned with. Yet once again, the men leave her alone.

What do these women have in common? They have so much; what is it they lack? Why is it they may be able to hook a man but can't hold him? The women puzzle over this quandary themselves. They gather at professional clubs, sorority meetings or over coffee at the office and wonder what's wrong with black men? They hold special prayer vigils and fast and pray and beg Jesus to send the men back to church. They find the brothers attending political strategizing sessions or participating in protests, but when it comes time to go home, the brothers go home to someone else.

I know these women because I am all of these women. And after asking over and over again "What's wrong with these men?" it finally dawned on me to ask the question, "What's wrong with us women?" What I have found, and what many of these women have yet to discover, is that the skills that make one successful in the church, community or workplace are not the skills that make one successful in a relationship.

Linear thinking, self-reliance, structured goals and direct action assist one in getting assignments done, in organizing church or club activities or in positioning oneself for a raise, but relationship-building requires different skills. It requires making decisions that not only gratify you, but satisfy others. It means doing things that will keep the peace rather than achieve the goal, and sometimes it means creating the peace in the first place. Maintaining a harmonious relationship will not always allow you to take the straight line between two points. You may have to stoop to conquer or yield to win.

In too many cases, when dealing with men, you will have to sacrifice being right in order to enjoy being loved. Being acknowledged as the head of the household is an especially important thing for many black men since their manhood is so often actively challenged everywhere else. Many modern women are so independent, so self-sufficient, so committed to the cause, to the church, to career or their narrow concepts that their entire personalities project an "I don't need a man" message. So they end up without one. An interested man may be attracted, but he soon discovers that this sister makes very little space for him in her life. Going to graduate school is a good goal and an option that previous generations of blacks have not had. But sometimes the achieving woman will place her boy-friend so low on her list of priorities that his interest wanes. Between work, school and homework, she's seldom "there" for him, for the preliminaries that might develop a commitment to a woman. She's too busy to prepare him a home-cooked meal or to be a listening ear for his concerns because she is so occupied with her own.

Soon he uses her only for uncommitted sex since to him she appears unavailable for anything else. Blind to the part she's playing in the problem, she ends up thinking, "Men only want one thing." And she decides she's better off with the degree than the friendship. When she's forty-five, she may wish she'd set different priorities while she was younger. It's not just the busy career girl who can't see the forest for the trees.

Couples I know were having marital troubles. During one argu-ment, the husband confronted the wife and asked what she thought they should do about the marriage, what direction they should take. She reached for her Bible and turned to Ephesians. "I know what Paul says and I know what Jesus says about marriage," he told her, "What do you say about our marriage?" Dumbfounded, she could not say anything.

Like so many of us, she could recite the Scriptures but could not apply them to everyday living. Before the year was out, the husband had filed for divorce. Women who focus on civil rights or commu-nity activism have vigorous, fighting spirits and are prepared to do whatever, whenever, to benefit black people. That's good. That's necessary. But it needs to be kept in perspective. It's too easy to save the world and lose your man.

A fighting spirit is important on the battlefield, but a gentler spirit is wanted on the home front. Too many women are winning the battle and losing the home. Sometimes in our determined efforts to be strong believers and hard workers, we contemporary women downplay, denigrate or simply forget our more traditional feminine attributes. Men value women best for the ways we are different from them, not the ways we are the same. Men appreciate us for our grace and beauty. Men enjoy our softness and see it as a way to be in touch with their tender side, a side they dare not show to other men. A hard-working woman is good to have on your committee. But when a man goes home, he'd prefer a loving partner to a hard worker.

It's not an easy transition for the modern black woman to make. It sounds submissive, reactionary, outmoded, and oppressive. We have fought so hard for so many things, and rightfully so. We have known so many men who were shaky, jive and untrustworthy. Yet we must admit that we are shaky, jive and willful in our own ways. Not having a husband allows us to do whatever we want, when and how we want to do it. Having one means we have to share the power and certain points will have to be surrendered. We are terrified of marriage and commitment, yet dread the prospect of being single and alone.

Throwing ourselves into work seems to fill the void without posing a threat. But like any other drug, the escape eventually becomes the cage. To make the break, we need to do less and "be" more. I am learning to "be still and know," to be trusting. I am learning to stop competing with black men and to collaborate with them, to temper my assertive and aggressive energy with softness and serenity. I'm not preaching a philosophy of "women be seen and not heard." But

I have come to realize that I and many of my smart and independent sisters are out of touch with our feminine center and, therefore, out of touch with our men.

About a year ago, I was at an oldies-but-goodies club. As a Washingtonian, I love to do the bop and to hand dance styles that were popular when I was a teen. In those dances, the man has his set of steps and the woman has hers, but the couple is still two partners and must move together. On this evening, I was sitting out a record when a thought came to me. If a man were to say, "I'm going to be in charge and you're going to follow. I want you to adjust your ways to fit in with mine." I'd dismiss him as a Neanderthal. With my hand on my hip, I'd tell him that I have just as much sense as he does and that he can't tell me what to do. Yet, on the dance floor, I love following a man's lead. I don't feel inferior because my part is different from his, and I don't feel I have to prove that I'm just as able to lead as he is. I simply allow him to take my hand, and I go with the flow.

I am still single. I am over thirty and scared. I am still a member of my church, have no plans to quit my good government job and will continue to do what I can for my people. I think that I have a healthy relationship with a good man. But today, I know that I have to bring some of that spirit of the dance into my relationship.

Dancing solo, I've mastered that. Now I'm learning how to accept his lead, and to go with the flow.

CHAPTER 5

▼

TALK TO ME—
RESPONSES
ABOUT THE ARTICLE

Female—Divorced—30's

I've seen the article before. While I don't dispute the fact that the home should be a safe haven, I find it very disheartening though (the article) because she's saying (to me) that women are the only ones in the relationship who have to sacrifice a part of themselves in order to be with someone. Why are men not made to step up their game and bring as much softness to the table as women? Am I not just as tired, just as stressed, just as drained? Why can't we both agree to be a little softer? It's sad when women have to make excuses for why they are still single instead of saying … I like being single. I like having my own space … and when I chose to be in the company of a man (be it a night, weekend or a year), I will, but without sacrificing who I am and what I need.

*   *   *   *

Male—Divorced—40's

The person that wrote this article hit the nail right on the head. I'm pretty sure there will be many Black women that won't agree and will say that Black men need to step up their game, take charge in their relationships, and not go running off into the arms of the white female!

In my personal experiences I've noticed that most Black females love to dominate the relationship. She will test the Black male's position in the relationship and in many cases she wants to lead the relationship. A relationship **is** like dancing in many ways. I have danced with many women who've said to me, "I like the way you lead, the way you make me feel when we dance together, and then there are the women that when I take their hands I can tell what kind of woman they are (dominating and controlling) and they want to lead the dance.

I want to be the man in my relationship! I want to have the last word. Not to just say yes/no, but that I know where I stand in the relationship. I have never put my woman or family in a bad situation, ever! I would give my life to protect my family! I think I deserve the right to have the last word and not be contested. Finally, a woman that has more education makes more money or has a perceived higher status neither bothers nor intimidates me.

*   *   *   *

Female—Single—40's

I think she is full of it. She is basically saying a woman should, not have a mind or thought of her own. I have no problem with the Man leading, if he knows how. To blindly follow someone knowing they are wrong is just stupid. A woman is supposed to be a man's "helpmate". So he to should be willing to except help at times.

*   *   *   *

Male—58—Divorced

This article makes some very good points, although I do take exception to some. I noticed that it started with how successful some women are but they still have problems with relationships.

Well, what do professional and personal accomplishments have to do with a relationship between a man and a woman? It might be impressive initially in the dating phase, but at home its all about how a man and woman relate to each other based on their personalities. No matter how successful a man or woman may be, you have to put that aside when you go home and start from ground zero. A woman can rationalize how men are threatened by her success and can't handle it, maybe this is so with men with low self esteem, but in many cases it's just an excuse to not look within yourself and deal with your issues. The statement 'you will have to sacrifice being right in order to enjoy being loved'.... sounds condescending ... it kind of sounds like deep down (the author of the article) does not have a high opinion of men. We all have to make allowances at times, it's a human thing. Being acknowledged as head of the household because a black man's manhood is challenged in society'.... is a bunch of crap ... my sense of manhood comes from within. I do not need to be acknowledged as the head, just treat me with respect (and vice versa).

One another point, there are many differences between men and women, but one is what attracts us. In my opinion, women are impressed by finance, accomplishments, power, etc.... along with looks (to a lesser degree than men). While men in many cases are attracted by intimacy (alright.... sex) ... this is very important to a man! Sex (intimacy) has a lot to do with how he feels about himself ... makes him feel alive. At the same time, this pursuit of intimacy has a very negative effect on women, makes many of them feel disrespected. So women seem to hold it over a man's head, use it as a reward or incentive (or punishment by withholding it). I don't know the solution to this issue, but I do know that it is very, very important to be desired, without it you have nothing to work with. These are just some of my opinions; I cannot speak for all men.

*   *   *   *

Female—Single—40's

I definitely can see this Sister's point and agree with much of what's she saying. I've been doing some observing myself and agree that many Sisters are emasculating our men, which is neither a good thing nor a smart thing. Nor is it fair to imply that only Black women do this to Black men, because it's an unfair statement. Unfortunately, most women don't see this, and I'll admit it's a revelation that came to me a few years ago!

I've had a CHANGE in my position about "not needing a man!" I was *kind of wrong*! I do need and want a man. However, I don't need a man for the "material" things that people strive for. I've been blessed with the ability to purchase a lovely home, my car is paid for and God has blessed so that I am able to supply my basic needs!!

However, I do need and want a man for the following:

- Companionship
- To explore new things with and travel with.
- To love me and for me to love!
- To go to church and worship with and to pray with and for me.
- To hold my hand during tough times and times of uncertainty.
- To be my best friend.
- To challenge me to be more than I even think I can be.

In return, I'm willing and desiring to give the same and more!!

I can't and won't change the things I've been able to accomplish in my life or the fact that I own my own home, have done some traveling and have worked to achieve the nicer things life has to offer. I don't believe a man should expect a woman to downplay her accomplishments just to soothe his ego! Nor do I believe my accomplishments need to be constantly thrown in his face.

Now if a man is "scared" to step up to a woman because of her accomplishments, we can't help that … that's his issue to deal with.

I think most of the women I know don't have an expectation that a man has to earn as much or more than us, because the reality is many don't. I know there are lots of wonderful men who have good jobs and work hard everyday. We really aren't overly caught up in that mindset, but you best believe the man better be gainfully employed and no, we will not put up with a lot of unnecessary drama!

*   *   *   *

Male—Single—50's

The article was too over simplistic. I didn't like it. "A fighting spirit"? There is much more to this issue than that. I suspect Ms. Jones is pretty young or had an editor who's watched too much "Sex in the City."

Read this book: "*Black & Single—Meeting & Choosing a Partner Who's Right for You*". Author—Larry E. Davis—It will offer much more effective insights into these issues than I ever can.

My number one rule: "Women are not allowed to violate my serenity." I want as little conflict or drama as possible in life, and I have absolutely no patience for this (unnecessary drama) in romantic relationships. However, if there is tension or disagreement, my first instinct is to check myself. In dealing with conflict in the family, I find usually that I am the problem and thus have no issue with adjusting. My sisters are wiser, more generous, more understanding, and often smarter than I am, and it is in my best interest to adjust in the pursuit of being a better person. "In the streets," the only sisters who usually have a clue are those with successful, happily married parents. I (along with many of my male friends) have maintained a belief that usually, women from two-parent households tend to have healthier perspectives on relations and the requirements to give and take to make a relationship work.

✳   ✳   ✳   ✳

Male—Divorced—50's

I break down the male mindset regarding relationships in the following categories:

1. **Ego & Time are on my side**—this was me at one time in my life. Frankly, there are 3 or 4 women that I have known that I am confident would have been great life partners for me. There is no particular reason for this position; it's just man's view of his opportunity at the time. After all, men are taught to be patient, "never make your move too soon" and all that. There is a certain degree of selfishness here that doesn't often view women as partners, but as people that want something from us. Our strength is expressed in holding back. Even in letting that "perfect partner" get away. I know that doesn't happen on TV, but remember that TV isn't real. There is ready validation out there. Most of our friends have done

the same thing—several times over—and they are still having a good time. Besides, my "man juice" (which women want) will still be flowing into my 70's—well that is some of the attitude.

For the record, guys don't mind having kids. Most guys even want them. We don't however, see children as "prizes" like many women do. We don't see children as income protection for when we get older, as some women do. And men, with half a brain, don't see having a child with a woman as a way of keeping her in his life—as many women do. These men are often the more educated.

2. **Fear**—Some guys are plain fearful of anything they cannot control, especially another woman. They are fearful of the unknown. Chances are the man has never seen a healthy male/female relationship.

3. **Just not ready now**—This is a "cousin" to "fear." These guys are not on the same path/in the same world as you are. Maybe they always have "something they want to do or accomplish" then they'll be ready. Of course, they'll never attain that "thing." That "thing" is good to hide behind. Maybe they'll get comfortable some day, not today. When they do, these guys are always happy as a lark. After all, they've been rescued.

4. **"Poor" Mentality**—Some people, no matter what their station in life, no matter what they have achieved, no matter how much education they have (I know surgeons, anesthesiologists, psychologists, teachers, politicians, judges, entrepreneurs and executives like this, so do you), no matter how much money they have, they will always be "poor." Being poor is a state of mind. Being poor for many people causes them to build walls from others. However, in reality—that same wall prevents them from ever getting out.

As much as I hate to say this, I believe the problems (gap) between men and women are getting worse.

- Guys don't want to raise another man's children, yet out-of-wedlock births are at an all-time high.

- Teenage guys dating girls with at least 2 kids is common.

- Parents are not investing in their kids. In my view there are 2, and likely 3, full generations of Black parents that have failed their children. The trend is in the wrong direction. Peddle to the metal in the wrong direction.

✳   ✳   ✳   ✳

Female—Divorced—40's

I can relate to the article only to a certain point. All the relationships I have been in, I <u>have</u> shown the "soft side" and don't talk about business—I believe I possess all that men say they are looking for (the complete package). Only when I am asked to share, have I done so. It seems the guys seek out the professional information on women and when they realize what they have, they then realize they are not up for the work/effort on the other side. Only to realize that they really don't have to work hard at all. I also have learned that most of the Black men (professional) are not used to dealing with women of higher standards and accomplishments even though they say that that is what they want. When they get it, they want to take you back to the "Neighborhood." I do not agree with sisters taking all the blame.

I think that both sides (men and women) need to write down what they really want and leave those of us who are happy alone. I love me some Black men, but the others are starting to look really nice. I have decided <u>not</u> to limit myself to just Black men. There are some really nice Caribbean and Latin guys out there, too.

* * * *

Male—Divorced—50's

It's interesting that more men have responded about your comments (thus far). I also forwarded it to some other women. One became defensive and stated that she was just fine with her "smart and independent" female friends.

I informed her that her statement was one of the reasons why she and her "smart and independent" female friends don't have a man (Black, White or otherwise), nor will they be able to keep a man because they think they "know it all."

I also told her that we (men), already know that you (Black women), are smart and independent. We just don't need to be told that all the time (like every day). I believe most men know a dumb and dependant woman when they see her.

It is so hard to dialogue with some of us nowadays, because no one really wants to "hear" what the other person is saying.

* * * *

Female—Married—40's

I read the article and feel it is more of the same. Each of us, (women) have gifts and the true answer is allowing God to place the one that He has created for us into our lives. I believe if he is God's choice he will accept me as I am. I will not need to concentrate on being submissive or whatever. The man for me will know how to guide and I will with the help of God instinctively know how to follow. Too much thinking and trying to fix the problem rather than truly and completely putting it in the Fathers hands. This is not easy for it may mean waiting alone for many years.

$$* \quad * \quad * \quad *$$

Female—Single—50's

Hmm, interesting food for thought. While Ms. Jones makes some valid points, I believe some men do use this point "smart (strong) black women" as an excuse to not commit to a relationship! Others feel threatened by the woman's success. We do, however, have to ask ourselves, "are we too independent?"

$$* \quad * \quad * \quad *$$

Male—Married (10+ yrs)—40's

I've heard of this before. I've never feared a woman fitting this description, especially not now. Being a heterosexual man, I have a tremendous love for women, the thorn in my flesh you might say, and God has blessed me to remain faithful to my wife.

I would never be repelled by a woman with such positive attributes. In fact, I've been married to one for over 10 years now and I do experience some of the problems described here. She's not very traditional, it doesn't come naturally for her at all and it's been a huge struggle for us. For her to do stuff like washing, ironing, cooking, cleaning, preparing lunch, it's just not innate. She is better, but has a way to go.

As crazy as this sounds, if I could do marriage all over again, I would not mind at all having a woman like this, however, I'd take more time before marrying to make sure I don't encounter the same challenges I'm experiencing now.

*   *   *   *

Female—Single—40's

My first thoughts were that this is nothing new. Our parents and grandparents did this for years with their man. But, obviously they must have seen a flaw with it, because they instilled within us to be independent women. It seems this article is suggesting that women have to make a full circle in order to achieve successful relationships with men. I disagree.

I feel just as there are intelligent, smart and business savvy women who have learned the art of achieving a good life for themselves; there are also equally smart men. I feel with a combination of intellect and social skills, the two should know how to communicate and compromise to make a relation work. I think it is working gradually but it took awhile for our generation to catch on.

"In too many cases, when dealing with men, you will have to sacrifice being right in order to enjoy being loved." If you have to sacrifice your morals, values and whom you are to be loved, then you are not being loved for who you are.

"Many modern women are so independent, so self-sufficient, so committed to the cause, to the church, to career or their narrow concepts that their entire personalities project an "I don't need a man" message." Most women don't and the sooner they realize that, the better they will become. The Bible said that when a man finds a woman, he finds a good thing. Men need to realize how good and valuable women are to them, and it's a blessing from God. When men realize that, they will respect the woman in such a manner that not only is she of value to him but also her opinion.

"Couples I know were having marital troubles. During one argument, the husband confronted the wife and asked what she thought they should do about the marriage, what direction they should take. She reached for her Bible and turned to Ephesians. "I know what Paul says and I know what Jesus says about marriage," he told her, "What do you say about our marriage?" Dumbfounded, she could not say anything. Like so many of us, she could recite the Scriptures but could not apply them to everyday living. Before the year was out, the husband had filed for divorce. Women who focus on civil rights or community activism have vigorous, fighting spirits and are prepared to do whatever, whenever, to benefit black people. That's good. That's necessary. But it needs to be kept in perspective. It's too easy to save the world and lose your man."

These two people were just simple unequally yoked. I agree many people tote the Bible and quote scriptures, but I believe if you truly believe what you say you believe in, then you will be committed to it. This couple was not committed and had no solid foundation to build the marriage on. If they did, the Bible, "what Paul said", "what Jesus said", would have been enough to make the marriage work. It seems the husband wanted out just as much as the wife did and both are equally to blame.

"A hard-working woman is good to have on your committee. But when a man goes home, he'd prefer a loving partner to a hard worker."

I agree, but if a man is secure in whom he is, he can appreciate a woman a hardworking woman in one respect and a soft a gentle woman in another. There is no reason why a woman cannot be all that she is to be. She should not behave in a certain manner that will project who she is not or make her uncomfortable in order to satisfy someone else. By doing so, she would be loosing her identity. A secure individual can accept a person for all of who they are. We all have different roles to play at sometime or another, and it should be viewed as such.

I agree with the article in respect that in a relationship or partnership, all parties should have roles and responsibilities. There will be leaders and followers, and marriage is no different. However, a responsible person cannot sit idly by and follow a bad leader. Therefore, marriage is no different. The husband needs to be a good leader and lead by example. He cannot assume this position by default (because he is a man) and expect to be good at it and have a submissive following wife. I don't believe that is not in God's design for marriage.

*   *   *   *

Female—Single—40's

Creating and maintaining a successful relationship and/or marriage is like a 2nd career—it requires work and a sincere commitment! Unfortunately, most folks work harder at their "day" jobs than they do their marriages or relationships. Think about it! People put in the time necessary to keep their jobs to get that promotion. They'll stay late or come in early if need be. They'll even come to work "sick as a dog" just to complete a project on time. They'll go to training to learn the latest tools & sharpen the necessary skills, so they can stay at the top of their game, stay competitive and advance. They'll even sacrifice time with their families and friends for the job.

Too few couples put that type of effort into working on and maintaining their marriages/relationships.

*   *   *   *

Female—Single—30's

I read that ... very good article! Have no comments other than I agree with some points, others are questionable ... Everyone's "case" is different, different frames of reference, different nuances.

The one "commonality" I can get with is this: Many people are terrified of marriage and commitment, yet dread the prospect of being single and alone. Admittedly ... that would be in my "profile" if you will!

*   *   *   *

Female—Divorced—50's

I am ashamed to admit that often, I have considered not doing things in my career because of the very fear of having too much for some men to handle.

I think the article is valid; however, I'm unsure how to correct or unsure I have a willingness to play into the whole thing. I want someone to get to know me and all of my frailties and strengths, however. I struggle how to combat first impressions.

*   *   *   *

Female—Married—50's

Why do we have to be lead? We are intelligent beings capable of thinking and decision making. I shouldn't need to be in a relationship so bad that I have to check my brain at the door! The cost of peace and love can become too high! How much does a sister have to pay for love? I disagree with Ms. Jones.

*   *   *   *

Female—Divorced—30's

I have a problem with the course the author has taken. While she makes valid points on varied issues, her overall message is a bit flawed. From the dawn of time the woman has been the one that sets the tone of a relationship and the household. A strong woman can do it all. A Superwoman should be able to make her mate feel loved (if he understands the direction of the relationship) and be attentive to the kids, run a company and participate in the church. There is no reason a woman should ever give up her goals and dreams. If a man does not understand that I may only have 1 hour to spend with him on Tuesday night, then he must not have any goals or he has already achieved his. Either way, it's his problem. I agree with the author that a relationship should not be a competition, but a team effort; and if my team has 2 master's degrees rather than one, shouldn't that make the team stronger? The goals and decisions (whether they are personal or professional) should be for the benefit of the team.

I do agree with the author's comment that the skills that make one successful at work are not the necessarily the same set of skills needed to make a relationship successful. There is a lot of give and take and sometimes more take than give that occurs in a relationship. I don't have the "I don't need a man" complex. I am willing to compromise. Every woman is not like the author, some just got dealt a bad hand. We should not attempt to bucket all the sisters that don't have a man into an overall "what did we do wrong" category. I think women and men should work to achieve all the goals they set; and if they are a workaholic or a career student or a super-mom, (unless you select a mate that understands you and appreciates who you are as a person), the relationship will be very difficult to develop or maintain.

✳   ✳   ✳   ✳

Female—Divorced—50's

It certainly made me think. I can recognize parts of myself in this article. I got some interesting reactions when I forwarded the article. One guy friend of mine responded by telling me "this is so not you." I appreciated his support, but I truly am an independent, tough, aggressive woman. The thing is, "it is who I am." Part of it comes from the fact that I've had to take care of myself for a very long time. I didn't get married until I was 35 years old. After living on my own and moving up as a corporate professional, it's hard to shrug that off and become needy and dependent. I do mellow out when I'm in a relationship (from the best of my memory—it's been so long since I was in one). I compromise and negotiate (these are skills you need in management, too). I coo and cuddle and I'm very affectionate. I don't have to be in control; in fact, I love it when a man takes charge. But I will still maintain a level of independence.

*   *   *   *

Male—Married—40's

I'm not sure I agree with everything she says, but I think the overarching theme is that your mate should be your number one priority. The basic tenants of a successful relationship are pretty straight forward: trust, compromise, sacrifice, etc. The difficult part is doing it. It is not easy, however. Relationships are an individual thing; there is no one set formula.

*   *   *   *

Female—Married—30's

I could never be "the background" to anyone's "foreground," and I don't believe you should have to in order to keep or obtain a man. I am extremely strong willed and tend to attract quiet-although strong men. A man has to be secure in himself in order to obtain a woman who will respect him. In saying that, I think women lowering their standards (not "being there or not having enough time for") have contributed more to the moral decay of the black relationship than anything. Just as we "take them (men) as they are," they (men) should do likewise. I'm not saying I've never held my tongue or been supportive of an idea that I really didn't approve of; I'm just stating this is not the basis of the relationship, nor is it the glue that binds the relationship together. When we refuse the blessings God has for us and sacrifice being ourselves in the name of having relationships, who are we fooling besides ourselves? A man that truly wants a woman, wants one with her own opinion, goals, and dreams—to dream with him, not someone that has to stifle what should truly be hers to be with him.

*   *   *   *

Male—Married—30's

This is a very good article. The writer is on point! If she is actually living by the words she writes, she's well on her way to a healthy relationship. However, I would add the one thing she fails to mention is that the success in relationships is dependent on the "giver" and the "receiver"(whose roles seem to change hourly).

The real key is for both parties to let their guards down and get to know the things that are important to their mate, be willing and know when to bend, and last, but not least, make each other the first priority (after God). The right man will know when it is important for him to lead as well as when he should share that responsibility with his woman. The right woman won't have a problem "dancing" (i.e. as referenced in the article) her way to and through a happy relationship or marriage!

*   *   *   *

Male—Married—50's

True happiness is not about being single or married. If you are not happy from within as a single person, you won't be happy when married. I have been married now for over 20 years and it is great! I love my wife more than I ever have, but I believe I can give love to my wife and children because I learned to love myself long ago when I was young. For me it was being raised in a Christian home that planted my spiritual seed. Now that I have allowed the Spirit of Jesus Christ to rule my life, marriage, work, social life, etc. are all dictated by my relationship with Christ.

Rather than spend so much time and energy pursuing a mate for marriage, people should use their time of singleness to work on themselves so that they grow to be happy with themselves first. Once that's achieved, it will be much easier to be happy with someone as well as accepting of another.

*   *   *   *

Male—Married (20+ yrs)—50's

The problem I have with the article is that it appears the author (woman) feels the need to become someone she's not in order to have the relationship she desires. No one can work at a relationship or more importantly, have a successful relationship if they're pretending to be someone they aren't. I further think the author of the article or anyone will not like the person they became just to get a mate. If you're going to fight me ... fight me from day one and let me/us decide if the relationship (person) is worth the effort. Over time, the person who changed and is no longer true to themselves, will grow to resent the person they've become and the sacrifices they feel they made to have (and maintain) the relationship, not to mention resent the person they made the changes for ... then the real drama begins!

✳   ✳   ✳   ✳

Female—Married—40's

I fell in love with my husband the minute I saw him and told him so when we finally met. He gave me my **wedding** band on our third date. We dated for 12 years before we **married** and I wouldn't trade him for all the tea in China. What **makes** it work is the respect we have for the other and that we do everything for each other. I have no problem cooking and serving him **dinner**. Other's say I do too much, but in return he helps with my **family**, runs the vacuum and cleans the oven! He is my first thought and I believe I am his. Give in to giving from your heart not your mind. What others think is not important when the day is done. Remember, High Expectations Yield Great Rewards.

✳   ✳   ✳   ✳

Male—Married (5+ yrs)—30's

I will say that this Sister is on the right track. It begins with her accepting God's master plan and design for women and men. Then introspection helps put it into a personal context. Prayer blankets it. Then the blessings come.

My wife and I have six years behind us (and a lifetime to go)! God is the apex and one of us is at each end of the balancing board. We work continuously on calibrating and recalibrating our balance.

Our theory is as follows:

• Priority 1—Please and glorify God with our relationship

- Priority 2—Focus on our commitment to Him and each other
- Priority 3—The remaining priorities fluctuate

*   *   *   *

Female—Married (20+ yrs)—40's

I will give you my opinion as a person who has been married over 20 years and in, what I consider, a good relationship. One thing we do is work together in all facets of our lives. You have to build a relationship and it is give and take, not one-sided. I didn't like the overall tone of the article because it seemed to imply that the woman must underachieve to get and keep a man. Why can't a man and woman work together and achieve individual and collective goals? That's what my husband and I do. No, it's not easy; but it surely is worth it. He fully supported me when I went back to school to get my M.B.A. I fully supported him when he decided to change careers and had to go away for two months for training. Was I happy about him getting into dangerous situations due to his new career? No, but I knew that's what he wanted. Marriage and any relationship require give and take on both sides. If a man has issues with a successful woman, then shame on him!

*   *   *   *

Male—Separated—40's

I really enjoyed reading this article and can relate to a lot of the points it made. In spite of all the advances we have made as a people, the black male-female relationship is still full of drama. We all know about the "Men are from Mars ..." thing that makes us see things differently; but in the African American community, men and women have to get on the same page.

First of all, I am not intimidated by a sister that has a good job/career, nice home, makes more money than me, and overall has her "stuff" together. No hater here! I know how hard she probably had to work and sacrifice to get to that position. So did I! In fact, that would be my preference. Not because I am looking to sponge off her for anything. But it is nice to occasionally have a woman say "hey, I've got the tab this time." Compare that to "I need some help on my rent ... again, because my baby's daddy is tripping." You feel me?! But seriously, nothing in this world worth having comes easily! This is just as true on the relationship front as it is on the material side. It is great when a sister is independent, confident and secure.

That being said, Sister's have got to let the man be the man! Show some love and support for a brother who is out there trying to do the right thing. If he works hard, loves you, loves his kids, and is overall a good person, then show him some appreciation. When he screws up, and he will, don't cut a brother to the floor. Show some understanding. Sisters have a habit of seeming to forgive, but never quite forgetting. The next argument, she brings up stuff that a brother did a year ago. Either let it go, or let him go. You can't have it both ways. A sister will get mad about seeing a brother walking down the street with a white woman or any other ethnic group. But when a brother stops to hold/open a door for a sister, she'll walk through it with not even a "thank you" if she doesn't deem the brother worthy.

CHAPTER 6

▼

WHO IS JOY JONES?

If you're like me, you probably want to know who Joy Jones is.

Joy Jones is a nationally known and recognized trainer, keynote speaker, playwright, and performer. Joy's innovative and interactive sessions in cross cultural communication, cultural diversity, career planning, creativity, and African American culture and history provide participants with opportunities for new growth and learning.

Ms. Jones spent 12 years as an educator, trainer, and administrator with the D.C. Public School System. She also designed the communication curriculum and trained for Wider Opportunities for Women's Nontraditional Work Programs. Her articles and essays have appeared in *The Washington Post, The Washington Times*, and many magazines. A live recording of Creativity and Spirituality, and an anthology of her performance poetry—Bad Beats, Sacred Rhythms—are available on audio cassette.

Ms. Jones' workshops include topics such as "Multicultural Standards of Beauty"; "She's Not in Your History Book"; "Creativity and Spirituality" and "Cross Cultural Communication." She is also the author of "Between Black Women: Listening with the Third Ear and Tambourine Moon," a children's book which honors her father. Joy's latest book, "Private Lessons: A Book of Meditations for Teachers," was published in 2001. Her plays have appeared on stages in Washington, New York, Pennsylvania, and California. Ms. Jones earned a BS in Communication, Magna Cum Laude from the University of Detroit.

CHAPTER 7

▼

HAVE WOMEN GOT IT WRONG?

This question has been coming up in my mind again and again … Could part of the problem be that women are "aggressively" searching for a non-existing Mr. Right? I think that is a big part of the problem and it is truly colorless.

Are too many women simply looking for a "Mr. Anybody" (warm body) to marry as soon as they can convince him that she's the one for him?

It seems to me that when women take on the role of searching for a husband (mate), one of two things happens: They realize Mr. Right never existed ~ (sorry!), any more than Ms. Right exists. They often fail to acknowledge (especially if the couple is talking marriage) until after the wedding and honeymoon are over or after the kids have arrived that they either settled, married someone they really didn't know or realized they weren't really "in love" with the man they married. They were probably far more in love with the notion of getting married … than being married. There is a huge difference, and I have often wondered if we really take the time to think about this.

Our society is a huge advocate of family, couples and being in relationships, which when you think about it, is perfectly natural. Our interest in who is or is not in relationship is sometimes too intrusive. Just look at how we all eat up (news) press on celebrities and their relationships. Who they're dating, who they could/might be dating, who broke up with whom, who married who, etc. We are insatiable! I'm guilty of this, too, as a regular reader of *"People Magazine."*

Being in a relationship can be a wonderful thing … it's the reason (I believe) we were created. In fact, it was never God's intent that we should be alone. The Good News Bible translates Genesis 2:18 this way: "Then the Lord God said "it is not good for man to live alone. I will make a suitable companion to help him." So, even God recognized the need for and importance of being in relationship with Him and with one another.

I don't know of anything that makes a person *"glow"* more than being in a positive, healthy, fulfilling and loving relationship with someone who truly loves, values and respects them back. I found a quote that I truly love and have it posted in both my home and office. It says: "The joy of being in a relationship that feels complete is that it honors and enriches both people every day." I interpret this to mean that I shouldn't settle for being in any relationship that I don't feel honored, cherished and happy in. Notice that I didn't say <u>makes me feel whole</u>. I'm a whole person now. I strongly believe we all need to be whole and complete people before we get into a relationship with someone. Expecting another person to make you whole or complete is way too much of a burden and an unfair responsibility to put on someone else. The reality is, no one can make another person whole or complete. They can enhance you, your life, but they cannot and should not be responsible for making you feel whole.

Where did the idea come from that if you are not in a "relationship" there is something wrong with you? That is totally incorrect and very dangerous thinking. Too many young adults and teens are buying into this mindset and hooking up with people who are toxic and totally wrong for them. They end up having sex too early, being in abusive relationships and taking crap from people totally unworthy of them.

So, here's my next question: "Why are women searching for their husbands?" There are women today (no ethnic groups exempted) who have every aspect of their wedding totally planned out from their wedding dress, to the cake, shoes, flowers, reception location, number of folks in the wedding, etc. The only thing missing is the groom. Think about how many women you've heard say … my wedding is going to be this or that. Doesn't it take two people to have a wedding and most importantly a marriage? So now, the chase is on—these women will date any and every body with the objective being that "every man" has the potential to be their husband and father of their child(ren), and the first man to pop the question (or think he's popped the question) will do. If you've ever seen the TV show (reality show) *Whose Wedding is it Anyway*, you'll see exactly what I'm talking about. I am totally amazed at how little attention and input most of the grooms have into the planning of the wedding.

Most of these women are so busy trying to have that perfect fantasy wedding (regardless of the cost), be the princess for the day (or several months if you include all the showers and parties) that they totally miss it. I strongly believe if couples would put as much effort and emphasis into their marriage as they did into planning the wedding (ceremony), people would be a lot happier and marriages would possibly last a lot longer."

I'm concerned that too many women (and perhaps men) are missing some important signals (possibly blaring warning signs) about a potential mate. The Bible says in Proverbs 18:22: "A man who finds a wife finds a good thing and obtains favor from the Lord". That's powerful! What does that say to you? To me it implies that it is the man who should be the one looking/searching for a wife or pursuing the woman. It should **not** be the other way around. Now saying that, I'm not at all saying women must or should accept every man that expresses an interest in **us**. I firmly believe that while the man should initiate the pursuit, women have the right to say yes or no to the pursuit. Every man who expresses an interest in you … ain't for you! My girlfriends have very often heard me say that "every man you meet and date ain't "the one." I have grown to realize (through trial and error) that when I date a man, I serve myself best to have no expectations that he will be the one or that one date will lead to a relationship. This takes the pressure off me and allows me to be myself and get to know the **man**.

CHAPTER 8

▼

THE SISTER-GIRL'S SESSION

OK, earlier, I mentioned that I hosted a Sister-Girl's Supper to discuss Ms. Jones' article. A group of fifteen women were invited and ten women ranging in age from forty to sixty showed up for food, fellowship and a very lively discussion. The break down of marital status of these women follows:

- Four are married (a couple on their second or third marriage)

- Four are divorced

- Two are single, never married

I'm very happy to report that there was no male bashing whatsoever! In fact, it was stated early on that the emphasis of the discussion had to be on us … as women and our stuff. The discussion lasted a couple of hours and when all was said and done, here's the gist of what was said:

The overall feeling was the women disagreed with the article. The feeling was that we are not scaring off our men; they're scaring themselves. Everyone agreed that the article was written to have women look at ourselves.

When discussing Ms. Jones' analogy of dancing (stepping or swing, where the man is required to lead), the feelings were unanimous that men and women have to learn to "dance" together. Learning someone's rhythm takes time. Many women have to learn to allow the man to lead in the dance and learn to recognize his "signals" while dancing … i.e. when to turn, when to move left or right, etc. Everyone also agreed that in order for women to successfully follow in the dance, the man needs to know (or be willing to learn) how to lead in the dance. It's hard to follow a dance partner (man), when you can't recognize his "dance" signals. If his hand movements are too "subtle," the woman struggles to understand what he needs her to do or which way he wants to move. If his movements are too forceful, she feels tossed about and as if she's being forced in her movement.

We need more spiritually mature men in healthy and loving relationships to take time to mentor young men and boys who have no real positive male role models ... share the knowledge! That's truly the only way these young men will learn how to be real men ... by interacting with other men in healthy relationships. No one can be what they don't know.

Everyone thought that it was important for women to look at themselves and do some "internal soul searching;" to see what (if anything) they can do to make a paradigm shift. This shouldn't require them to change who they are or diminish what they've accomplished, or what they believe in. However, this soul search should help them to understand how they respond to situations (men) and not be so quick to blame the man.

The women who were single and divorced all stated they do want to be in a committed relationship but disagree that they should have to "stoop" to have a relationship.

One woman said this discussion has put her in the mindset to do some soul searching of her own. Several women acknowledged they often responded to situations negatively, primarily because they react (respond) emotionally, rather than on what the real issue is (or is not).

CHAPTER 9

▼

FACING OUR STUFF

Now, doing this is going to force many of us (male and female) to do an honest analysis and really take some time to "look at our stuff!" This won't be, and often is not, pretty; in fact it can often be painful. Let's be honest, who wants to deliberately do something that is painful and brings up some bad memories or negative experiences. Further, this exercise will require us to open our hearts and minds to the possibilities that perhaps we do need to make "some" changes—large or small. I don't believe it's Ms. Jones' intent to have women change who we are, because people should be free to be who they are and have a relatively high expectation that people will accept us as we are ... but let's face it, we all have some issues and perhaps by taking some time and doing some honest introspective soul searching, we might find one or two areas in our personalities that could use some "tweaking" (I love that word)!

In the News

A friend sent me a series of articles that ran in the Chicago Sun-Times in 2005, dealing with male-female relationships. One article was titled "Searching for Mr. Right." One of the women interviewed had ended a very long-term (more than 5 years) relationship with a man she thought she'd marry. The article was interesting, but brought to my mind the following thoughts: She wanted to be married, but the guy chose not to settle down. You know where I'm going ... did they ever discuss the goals of the relationship? What each of them expected? Did she stay with him all those years because she truly loved him or because she hoped that if she hung in there long enough, he'd want to marry her? The other question that has to be asked is, "Could it be that while he may eventually want to settle down (marry), he didn't want to settle down with (marry) her?"

As I stated earlier, I think one of the biggest mistakes many women are making today is that they're out trying to catch the man. Let's face it; there are more single women out there than single (heterosexual) men. There are even television shows that are airing with the sole purpose of telling women "how to catch the guy." I think we're getting this wrong ... very wrong.

This goes back to what I said earlier (speaking from a biblical perspective) I believe it is God's intent for the man to find a wife ... not the other way around. I just don't believe that women are always being as objective as we need to be if we're the ones pursuing. I know a lot of women are probably not going to agree with me about this, but it's just how I feel. After a certain age, I believe that women are dealing with some serious issues ... one of the biggest is that we hear our biological "clocks" ticking so loudly that we often can't hear (or see) anything else! So now, if we don't have children but want children, and there is no significant man in our lives who can give us these children, we begin to feel the search must begin (with a full court press) to find a husband. Women begin to date men and look at each one from the mindset that every man has the potential to be "the one!" Now don't get me wrong, I personally think you should only seriously date someone you can see yourself being friends with. I think that as you "learn" a person, you can then begin to determine if this is someone you could see yourself in a more serious/committed relationship with. If you both discuss and determine this is the road you want to take, and you agree that you want to commit yourselves to a monogamous relationship, you can then spend time to see if this relationship is going in the direction that could possibly lead to a committed relationship and marriage. I heard this great analogy of seeing yourself married to someone: Is this the person I want holding my hand at the death of a parent or loved on?" Sounds a bit morbid, I know, but it's a powerful question. When I heard it, it made perfect sense to me. Think about it, if during one of the most emotional and life shattering events, can you count on that person to be there for you to lean on, to help carry you through this difficult time? To be able to step up and assume the lead, because they know that at this time, you're not able to move forward? If you can't answer "yes" to this question, then perhaps you need to reconsider and re-evaluate the relationship.

OK, OK … I know exactly what you're thinking … Who am I to say you're taking the initiative to find a husband is wrong? I realize people are different. But let me tell you a story. I know a woman who was about to turn 35. She wasn't married and had no children. As her birthday drew closer, she began to compare her life to her mother's and girlfriends who, by the time they turned 35, were either married and had children or were working on or had an advanced degree. She truly began to feel time was passing her by and so was the window of opportunity for her to become a wife and mother … so; the push was on to meet these personal goals … a husband and have a child!

While traveling for business, she met a man who lived in another state. Within a very short time (about four months), they had begun talking about marriage, but there were some realities she couldn't ignore. While this man did have a job, he didn't make enough money to really support himself, how could he support the two of them? If they were going to be married, the chances were high that she was likely the one who would relocate, thus, she'd have to find a job and that could take some time. He lived in an apartment, but she owned a home. Would they move into his apartment or buy a home together? Would he be willing to relocate to her city to live? Additionally, moving to be with her guy, she'd no longer have any family close by and would have to make new friends.

Because of her desire to be married and become a mother, she continued on in the relationship, however, she began to have a recurring dream. It was the day of her wedding and the church was packed full of family and friends from all over. As she was walking down the isle, with her father, she stopped midway turned to her father and told him she couldn't marry this man. This dream occurs three times.

But her biological clock was ticking loudly and she knew she wasn't getting any younger. She then had to ask herself if she was truly in love with this man, or was she more in love with the idea of being married and becoming someone's wife and ultimately a mother. It's a serious question and one that must be asked and answered honestly.

So she began to pray on this. She finally went to meet the family of this man and it was while she was there, she received the confirmation she was seeking, almost immediately upon arrival.

By the time she returns from meeting this man's family and spending time with him in his "world," she knows, without a shadow of a doubt, that she cannot marry this man. She again prays and seeks God's direction, and once being at peace with her decision, she tells her man that she can not marry him nor can she continue on with this relationship. To do so would be a huge mistake for both of them. She was convinced that if she did marry him, they would be divorced within a year. She realizes that she wants to be in love with the man she'll one day marry, not in love with the idea of being married. She realized she had to be true to herself and she had to be true to the answer she received from the Lord regarding this relationship. To do otherwise, would be detrimental to everyone! It was a tough gut wrenching choice, but ultimately, she had to be honest with herself.

So you're probably wondering what happened to the guy? He of course was disappointed, but he quickly got over the hurt and her, because he was married within a year after they broke up!

So what about the dream of becoming a wife and mother? Well, it seems to me that if you really want to be a mother, you can become a foster parent or adopt. I'm always amazed at the stories I hear of couples who struggle for years to have a child of their own and once they make the decision to adopt, to open their lives and home up to someone outside of themselves, within a short period of time after that, they become pregnant. I believe that this is part of God's divine plan. Once we are willing to look outside our wants and plans and open ourselves and lives up to reach out to someone else, God can, and often does, bless us with our initial "heart's" desires. You could also become a big sister and/or open your life to the children of your friends and family.

As far as being a wife, that will come when God sends the man you're suppose to marry, when you are ready to be married. You'll know, and it won't require any fixing or changing of yourself (or him) to become someone's wife.

If marriage doesn't happen, recognize that is OK, too! You are still a wonderful, "whole" person who has much to offer this world with your talents, your time, etc. Marriage does not validate who we are. Marriage does not make us whole or complete people. Marriage can enhance the quality of your life, that's true. Marriage is a wonderful thing, however, it requires daily work and I believe a daily renewed commitment to each other. If you die and never experience marriage, at least leave here having lived the very best, fullest and most complete life possible!

First Corinthians 13 speaks about love. Specifically, 1st Corinthians 13 verses 4 through 8 read: "Love is patient, love is kind. It does not envy, it does not boast, it is not proud. It is not rude, it is not self-seeking, it is not easily angered, and it keeps no record of wrongs. Love does not delight in evil but rejoices with the truth. It always protects, always trusts, always hopes, and always perseveres. Love never fails."

This scripture is often read during marriage ceremonies, which of course is very appropriate. However, I think we really need to begin applying these verses to our daily lives, whether single or married. If we can grow to the point of truly loving ourselves, loving our lives, loving our talents, gifts, friends, family and even those who have hurt us, in the context of this scripture, I am convinced we will be better people for it! Our lives will be more complete and richer. The drama in our lives will be less, and the amount of "baggage" we carry will be greatly reduced. Our sense of peace and contentment will increase and we will develop the ability to better love someone else because we would have learned how to truly love ourselves.

There are still many good brothers out here! Unfortunately, too many of our men are lost, walking through life with no real vision, direction or guidance on how to be a hard working, successful, man.

What's even more unfortunate is too many of them have never seen a real strong, Christian man. They've never seen a man go to work daily and come home to his family at the end of the day. They've never had a man to talk with them, teach them how to be a man or explain what it means to be a man. They've had no one show them how to respect themselves and their lives and to value their opportunity to get an education, to learn, work hard in school and set goals for themselves and then sacrifice to accomplish those goals and make their dreams a reality.

They've never seen a man on his knees, praying for himself and his family and seeking God's guidance and direction. They've never seen a man read the Bible and be a true man of God and be the head of his family.

They've never seen a real man treat a woman with respect, love or dignity. Chances are high that they've never seen a woman treat a man with sincere love, respect and dignity.

The sad reality is too many of our children have never seen a faithful, committed and loving marriage. Too many have grown up in homes where love, true agape (unconditional) love between a man and a woman was something they only saw on TV, i.e. *The Cosby Show, or My Wife and Kids or the Bernie Mac Show.* For too many of our children, a happy and successful marriage is a myth … or considered "old school." Marriage is not something that works, nor do they believe it is worth the effort, so they are choosing instead to live together, because it is perceived as being easier, less restrictive and if things don't work out, they can just leave, rather than stick it out and put forth the effort to work at and grow the relationship.

I've begun to wonder if this absence of healthy relationship role models is one of the reasons many of our men turn to women outside of our race. Could the perception be that these women are better equipped emotionally to support, nurture and encourage our men, because they've seen this demonstrated in their homes by their mothers towards their fathers, therefore, they know how to give that emotional support? While I hope that's not the case, I have heard too many African American men state this as one of the reasons they date outside of their race.

Anything worth having requires work, effort and commitment. Meaningful and loving relationships will require overcoming ups and downs, adversities, disagreements, etc. We are dealing with another person, someone who has their own thoughts, beliefs and ideas on how things should be done, which could be very different from you. Different is not necessarily a bad thing. We just need to learn how to blend the good of both people into one harmonious existence and know when to make compromises on the rest. I realize this is easier said than done!

I know as women, we want the supportive, loving affectionate man we so often see in the movies, on television or read about in books, but that's just not always our reality ... it's usually not anyone's reality. People can't give what they've never received. If a man has never seen sincere, unconditional love and affection demonstrated between a couple, he is not going to know how to give it. This doesn't mean he can't learn it, but it will take some time and a lot of effort and work. Often we can teach much better by our actions than by any words we speak.

If we demonstrate genuine love, affection and support towards our men, even when they're not always loveable, our "walk" can often make them pause and look at themselves and want to do better. Our role as women should be one of support and encouragement. I certainly recognize that just as many of our men don't know how to show or give love, the same is true for too many women also.

Too many women have never seen the same scenarios I described above either. Too many of us have only seen ourselves negatively portrayed in the media or music videos, falsely believing that if we allow ourselves to be undervalued, underappreciated and treated with no respect, we will eventually get the man and be happy. We are giving away our self respect and dignity.

CHAPTER 10

▼

LIVE FOR TODAY ... BUT DON'T SETTLE

In the mean time, what should you do? Live your life! I can't tell you how much it frustrates me to hear women say they can't wait to do something once they are married. Whether it is purchasing a home, traveling, whatever. Why can't you do it now? Who says you're even going to get married? Are you willing to allow life and opportunities for fun, adventure and happiness to pass you by all because you're waiting for a husband? Lord, I sure hope not.

The other thing that occurs is that women will settle for anyone just to say they're in a relationship ... or just to have a relationship. Now, don't confuse "settling" to mean being with someone who may not match you economically (financially). I'm not saying that. In fact, I think too many of us get caught up in the mindset that we have to be with a man who makes X amount of money, drives a certain type of car, owns a home, etc. yet many of us (this number is shrinking I must acknowledge) are not achieving these things for themselves.

What I'm trying to say is there are a lot of wonderful men who are blue collar workers that many women are not willing to consider. These men work hard every day, make a decent salary, possess the qualities we say we want in a man and like everyone else, want to be in a committed loving relationship.

I believe everyone needs to live their life as they know it ... this day, because this life on this day is all any of us truly knows. Your life as a wife and mother is a dream (especially if you're neither) and while dreams and fantasies are wonderful and can come true, they are not guaranteed. They could possibly become reality in the future; however, tomorrow is promised to no one.

If you have the desire to travel ... travel! Get involved in something. Make a difference! Focus on things other than the fact that you're not in a relationship, not married or a mother. I have found that when we take the focus off of ourselves, we can make a difference and God will always bless.

While writing this, another recurring thought has been running across my mind ... are African American women getting a bad rap?

I think we are in some ways and too often it's coming from too many of our men. They complain that we're too strong, too independent, expect too much and that our standards are too high for them (men) to achieve. They complain that we don't need them for anything. That's simply not true ... totally.

Are we strong? Yes we are. Can that strength be perceived as too assertive? Yes by some men. Do we have high expectations of and for the men in our lives? Yes. Those expectations are not only for the men in our lives, but they're for us as well. We have expectations for our children (if we have them) and families and friends. We want the best for them and we want the best for ourselves and our relationships. We want the people in our lives to recognize their own potential and strive to achieve the dreams they have for themselves.

Most of us are truly wonderful, hard working women who like most other humans simply want a loving and neutering relationship. We pray that God will bless us with that.

Perhaps we need to step back and focus on being the BEST person we can be to the people who are in our lives and strive to take care of ourselves. Nurture ourselves. Get healthy, exercise; find a hobby ... take care of yourself!

Be open to meeting men outside of our race if necessary. I truly believe that African American women are the last hold out for wanting to have a relationship with an African American man. By this I mean that we truly want to date and marry our men. Why is that? I think the answer is simple and something that too many of our brothers fail to appreciate. We truly appreciate and value our men! We know the talents and brilliance they posses. We appreciate their strength and their wisdom. We know that too often our men don't get a fair shake, and yes, we do push them, but we push them because we often times see the potential in them that too many of them fail to see in themselves.

I remember asking my mother when I was a teenager why she married my father. She listed a number of qualities she saw and liked in my father, but one of them has stayed with me all of these years. She said one of the reasons she married my father was because she saw the potential of the man he could become! I just really thought that was powerful. She believed in him! My father is a confident man, however, I know that my mother's belief in and support of him helped him to push forward and overcome during jobs lay offs, being overlooked for promotions and the many other challenges he's had to face as an African American man in this country.

CHAPTER 11

▼

DON'T BE SO QUICK TO KICK HIM TO THE CURB!

So, you've met someone. You've gone on a few dates and spent some quality time together and there are signs that this could possibly lead to something … but it doesn't work so you decide to no longer date each other.

So, what do you do? Do you just, kick him to the curb and totally out of your life? I don't think so … at least not always.

If we're really taking the time to get to know each other in the very early stages of developing a relationship (the friendship stage), perhaps if the "romantic" relationship fizzles, the friendship can survive…. even flourish!

Some of my best friendships are with guys I use to date. There's nothing physical (no sex) in the relationship, but we talk periodically, meet each other at the movies, have dinner, see a play and in some cases even play golf. I truly have no regrets about not being "romantically" involved with these men. They are truly wonderful men, but we, for various reasons, were just not "wonderful" together as a couple! I can honestly say that if I needed something, I could call on them and I'm confident they'd be there to help me and likewise, if they are in need … I'll help them.

Now let's be real, that "friendship" will not be developed or nurtured immediately after a breakup! We do need time to heal, get over the hurt and disappointment of the romantic aspect of the relationship not working, but given some time and soul searching (to see what role we played in the demise of the relationship), we can begin to build a friendship with that person. I truly believe men and women can be platonic friends.

Time really can heal most hurts and feelings. If we say that we want our significant other to first be our friend, then our boyfriend, the friendship should be the foundation. If not, perhaps we need to look at how we choose our friends.

Be very clear in your mind and heart that you no longer have any desire to become romantically involved with this person again and keep the relationship 100% platonic.

Male friendships can be very rewarding! Men are often a lot less petty about matters of the heart so they will usually tell it like it is ~ "straight with no chaser"! I always appreciate talking to my male friends about relationships because they come at things from a whole different perspective.

Our male friendships need to have a mutual respect. I believe we should treat our male friends like we'd treat our friendships with our girlfriends. What does that mean? It means that the relationship has to have balance and parity. When we hang with our girlfriends, we usually pay our own way. Once in a while we may treat each other, because of a birthday, promotion or some other special occasion, but for the most part, we each split things.

In our friendships with men, we shouldn't have the expectation that they are always suppose to pay, just because they're men, that's wrong and it is not fair.

Now there are some men, (although rare these days) who will insist on paying regardless ... that is just how they roll. I have a friend like that. Our friendship developed as a result of playing golf together. He would always pay for my round of golf (love that). Afterwards, we usually go eat. Initially, I offered to pay for dinner and he would always say no ... he's got it. This exchange went on a few times until he finally asked me "why did I always offer to pay for dinner?" I told him it was simple. He's paying for me to play golf and I didn't have the expectation that he should also pay for my meals too. I was willing to share the expense. I think my response surprised him, because he sat back and after a minute said that while he truly appreciated my offer and generosity, my money was no good with him and he didn't mind treating me! So ... who was I to argue with that! I do reciprocate in other ways. If I've cooked dinner, I'll cook extra so he can have couple of meals too! I also always make it a point to pack extra goodies for us to munch on while we're playing golf too. I acknowledge, he's truly a rare brother ... heck, he's a rare man period!

So, what's my point? My point is that friendships with men should be treated with the same level of mutual respect we have with our girlfriends. Don't treat a guy as your friend, yet have the expectation that he should treat you like his woman ... that friendship won't last long.

CHAPTER 12

▼

BEEN THERE ...
DONE THAT

As I was talking with women about my book and relationships, I've been noticing an interesting trend. It seems more and more women over forty who are single (usually through divorce) have no desire to remarry.

I wondered why and either directly asked or listened to women (yes, I was eaves-dropping) as they gave their reasons why they're done with the marriage thing.

The majority of these women have a wide range of outside interests. They play sports, in some cases where the woman hasn't physically had a child, she either has or is considering adoption. They have created fulfilling lives for themselves! These women are not spending their time crying about what they don't have, they're busy trying to achieve it!

For most of them, they stated that they've done the marriage thing and while it was nice, for awhile, they now have been divorced for so long and achieved a quality of life and life style they like, they can't imagine getting married and having to consider the feelings, or seek input from another person. Most of them have had their children and the kids are in college or close to college and it is now time for Mama to fulfill some of her personal dreams!

Many of these women do not want the emotional baggage being relationship brings. Some of them do not want to risk the pain and hurt of a relationship (or marriage) ending. That pain can feel overwhelming.

While home visiting the family, my brother introduced me to a man named Taki Ratan. Taki is the Founder and Principal of Blighton Delaney Academy in Milwaukee, Wisconsin. He's organized a number of workshops on male-female relationships and provides some very interesting insights in what African American men think about being in relationship with us. I realize Taki in no way speaks for all African American men, I do believe he communicates a lot of the thoughts I've heard and read from men.

According to Taki, his research shows that many women today are into "hooking up" or "slotting". These women want the excitement, enjoyment relationships often bring, however, they also want to maintain their independence and freedom. They are perfectly happy calling a man up when they want his company and companionship; however, they feel the need to run things.

Interestingly enough, while most of these women don't want to be married, many do appreciate having a significant man in their life to do things. Now the other twist is that many other women have no desire to be bothered at all with a relationship.

The majority of these women have a wide range of outside interests. They play sports, travel and do many things to enhance and enrich their lives. In some cases, where the woman hasn't physically had a child, she may be considering adoption or becoming a foster parent or volunteer as a big sister or mentor. The last thing these women are doing is spending their time crying about what they don't have, they're busy trying to achieve it!

CHAPTER 13

▼

SOME WORDS FOR THE FELLAS

I know what you're thinking … What is this woman about to say to us? Well, here it is … we need you! Who are we? Your women, your daughters and perhaps most critically, your sons! We are anxiously waiting for you to take the lead, to step up, however, we recognize that too many of you have never been shown how to step up and unfortunately, there are too many women who don't require that you have to.

Listen, women, regardless of race, cannot raise boys to become men. True there are women who are successfully raising their daughters and sons alone with no real positive male influence in their children's lives, but these children are truly missing out!

We need you to step up and be the fathers your father or grandfathers were. If you don't have a positive male role model that you can look to, then become the father and husband you WISH you're father would have been! The fact that you did not have this example growing up is no excuse for you to not become the best parent or husband you can. If you know better, you must do better! If you don't know how to go about becoming a better man, seek help. Go to church and get involved in their men's ministries, or if need be, start one of your own and seek out a minister or man in your church to be your mentor. Join organizations such a 100 Black Men (www.100blackmen.org) or the National Organization of Concerned Black Men, Inc. (www.cbmnational.org) or A Good Black Man (www.agoodblackman.org) or become involved with an organization called Project Fatherhood (www.fatherhood.org) or some other community service organizations in your area. Reach out!

If you are in a situation where you are not in the same house as your children, become involved in their lives! Even if there is baby-mama drama, stick it out and work through it. Never allow the issues you have with your child[ren]'s mother to stop you from having or maintaining a positive relationship with your kid(s). If that means you have to go to court, do it. If you're required to pay child support, pay it! Again, don't deprive your children. If you question that the money you pay is not going to meet the needs of your children, seek legal council to ensure your children have what they need … and then some.

It takes are real man to rear a child. D.L Hugley during one of his HBO comedy specials was talking about his stepfather and he made a statement that has stayed with me … he said "it takes a hell of a man to raise another man's seed". He truly credits his stepfather for raising him to be the man he is today. I think it was wonderful that he publicly acknowledged his stepfather and it was obvious that he truly loves and respects this man.

This generation of children is headed for extinction if you don't step up. We have too many young men in prison, unemployed and homeless. These young men and boys are crying out for guidance, direction and most importantly, love and they need these things from you!

The reality is this … any man can father a child, but unfortunately, not all men are fathers. During our discussion, Taki shared some disturbing statistics about the absence of Black father's in the home. According to some research by Dr. Jawanza Kunjufu, in the 1920's, 90% of African American fathers were in the home. By the 1960's this number was down to 80% and it is estimated that in 2007 only 37% of African American fathers are in the home. This means that 63% of African American men are MIA (missing in action)!

Taki acknowledges that Black men have played a large role in the demise of family in our community. Too many men are not stepping up to their God given roles as the head of their families. Perhaps this goes back to the points I made in Chapter 9 that too many of our men were never taught or shown how to be real men. Not knowing how to lead, support or care for themselves or their families.

Too many of our young men and boys too often see men "making babies" and then leaving either before or after the baby is born, leaving the sole responsibility of rearing and raising children to the mother.

They falsely and incorrectly think that's all they have to do, well, it is not! Perhaps a small part of the responsibility goes to the images our children see on television. Not just in music videos either, although they certainly do not help.

Unfortunately, the media and advertisers have begun to highlight the absence of Black fathers in the home. Are you even aware of the commercials that show the woman (usually African American) as the head of the household? One clear example of this was in two recruiting commercials for the U.S. Military. There were a couple of commercials that reinforce this unfortunate reality. The first one has an African American male teen at home with his mother eating dinner. He says he's made some decisions about his future and the camera pans down to his lap where he has some brochures on the military. He talks about his dream to become an engineer and how this particular choice can help him achieve this. The last line of the commercial has him saying, that it's time for him to become the man of the house.

The other commercial shows a young African American female who approaches her mother and is talking to her about her decision to join the military and is seeking input from her mother on her decision.

In both of these situations, the father is absent. There are certainly others, but these two are so specific and direct that it is worth noting.

Now, don't think I'm saying serving in the military is not an honorable profession, because I'm not saying that and you are totally missing the point. My point is that the father is totally absent from the dialogue. There is no input, guidance or direction being sought from him into the choices these young people are making for their future lives. In reality, there is no input, guidance or direction being sought from you by your children period ... this has got to change!

My brothers and I were blessed have had both of our parents under one roof growing up. As I mentioned earlier, they've been married nearly fifty years. We distinctly remember our father selling Girl Scout cookies and Boy Scout light bulbs, pizzas or whatever to his guys at work. Until he retired, my dad worked 3rd shift, so he was often the parent home when we left for school and on many days when we came home from school, he would have dinner started. When we were sick and Mom couldn't stay home with us, Dad was the care giver between the hours of 9am and 3pm.

For me, my father was the first man to validate me. Make me feel and believe I was worthy, important, smart, beautiful ... all of those things. He and my mother are my biggest cheerleaders. I am convinced that my relationship with my father growing up help to give me the confidence to be the woman I am today. Because of his presence, I am not seeking male approval or acceptance to feel worthy, I've had it all of my life.

I firmly believe it is absolutely critical for you as a father to be an active and positive participant in your daughter's life. Her relationship with you (or lack of relationship) will greatly impact not just how she looks at and relates to men, but also impact all of her future relationships with men. If she hears (from her father) that she is loved for who she is, respected and appreciated as a person, she will develop self worth and will have no need to seek this approval, love and acceptance from any ole man who comes along. You as her father, have the responsibility to give her that wonderful gift. The same holds true for your sons!

I have a friend who was divorced when his children were small and lived in another state. This man would do whatever he had to be a father to his children. That often meant driving through the night right after work to get there in time for a school function, father-daughter dance, basketball game, birthday, Christmas … whatever, he did it and I believe (and have told him this) that because of his efforts, God has blessed him to have a very strong and positive relationship with both of his children. That is something that no divorce, distance or anything can take away from you and your children. He was there to teach his son, how to be a man, how to treat women, instill a good work ethic, to be a sounding board and eventually to be his friend.

Another friend of mine calls his son an "endangered species". He recognizes that it is critical for him to nurture his son to become the man he is destined to be. To become the man God created him to be. He recognizes that while both he and his wife are important to his son's growth and development, only he can teach and more importantly show his son how to become a man!

CHAPTER 14

▼

CONCLUSION

It is my sincere hope that while reading this book; you have begun to have some personal dialogue with yourself to see where you stand. Once done (and keep in mind this should be an ongoing process), I hope you will begin to examine your role in your relationships or lack of.

I hope you will refer this book to others and that you can begin having some serious dialogue with your friends and loved ones about relationships, about your expectations and theirs. I pray that you will seriously seek God to provide you the truth and ability to face your own issues and to give you what you need to make the necessary changes in your life so that you can begin to receive the very best that God has for you and begin to live a life that is satisfying and ultimately be content with your life as you currently know it.

So, what's the next step? Put what you've read in this book into action! Go back and provide answers to the questions raised throughout this book. I don't believe there will be any wrong answers, but there will hopefully be honest ones. I hope you will be honest with yourself and search your heart and mind for some real honest answers for and about you.

If you are currently involved in a relationship (or think you are), how would you view the status of your relationship? Are you really in one or are you and that someone simply just kickin it and hanging out? Are you friends with benefits? Have you talked about if you both want to be in a long term relationship with each other? What does long term mean?

Is this someone you'd want by your side during the most trying times in your life, death of a parent, loss of a job, etc? Could you depend on this person to be there for you? Will this person have your back?

What if you are currently not in a relationship, are you OK with that? If not, why not? Why is it so important or critical that you be in a relationship?

What are your personal goals, beyond wanting a relationship? If you don't have any ... that's an even worse issue, and you need to set some. Go back to school, change jobs or careers, become active in your community, volunteer, travel, write a book, start a business, invest for your retirement. Look outside of yourself. How can your skills and talents benefit others?

Again, all of this requires some soul searching, but it is needed so that you can develop a life plan for yourself.

Write down your thoughts. Often times seeing your thoughts, goals and ideas on paper can help bring clarity and direction.

If you want to be in committed relationship, I believe it is important to write down what characteristics you want in a mate and pray for that. Be as specific as you think you need to be.

As I was doing my final edits for this book, I received news that a wonderful sister-girl friend passed away. The news of her passing rocked me as it was totally unexpected. I attended her home-going celebration which was beautiful and a true representation of her life. During the service, the minister extended a challenge to the congregation. He said, "don't waste your life being sad because you don't have love, instead, go out and be love!"

Be love to your family, friends, coworkers, children, within your community and even towards your enemies. Wherever you are, in whatever you do or say to others…be love! Let your walk demonstrate love. Let your words demonstrate love. Give the type of love you want in your life to the people in your life.

If we strive to live a life that is full and loving and not focused on what or who we don't have, we open our lives up to receive the very blessings we long for.

Once that's done, however, you must go about living your life as you know it today … not how you wish it could be in the future.

Strive to build a content and happy life for yourself. Not being concerned about what other people think you should be doing, or should have, but based upon what you believe will make you happy. Once you can clearly visualize this, the relationship stuff will take care of itself.

Your focus will be off of trying to find your "soul mate" because you will be busy living your life to the fullest and when God blesses you with the right person, you will also find the time and room in your life and heart and gladly welcome them into your world.

I haven't forgotten the fellas! Be present in the lives of your children. Remember they need you … just as we need you! We value, appreciate, love and believe in you and all that you are and are destined to be.

Strive to be the best man you can be for yourself and then your children. As I stated earlier, if you aren't sure or don't know how to do this, seek out a mentor. Read a book on fatherhood, become involved in a men's ministry or join a community organization. Surround yourself with people who will uplift, encourage and support you and most importantly who will hold you accountable to becoming the best man you can possibly be!

I would love to hear from you! To know your thoughts not just about this book, but also about the Joy Jones article and the responses shared by others in this book.

My email address is <u>cmdialogue@sbcglobal.net</u>.

I pray God's continued blessings upon you and that all of your hopes and dreams become your reality.

978-0-595-43502-9
0-595-43502-5

Printed in the United States
127845LV00003B/280-438/A